Christine Cole Catley

ℛ

RAVETTE PUBLISHING

Published by Ravette Publishing Ltd.
P.O. Box 296
Horsham
West Sussex RH13 8FH
Telephone: (01403) 711443

Editor – Catriona Tulloch Scott
Series Editor – Anne Tauté

Cover design – Jim Wire
Printer – Cox & Wyman Ltd.
Production – Oval Projects Ltd.

An **Oval Project** produced for
Ravette Publishing

For use of the objects on the cover
(a hand-carved Maori canoe bailer,
and a decorative headband)
grateful thanks are given to:

Kiwifruits
The New Zealand Shop
6 Royal Opera Arcade
London SW1

Contents

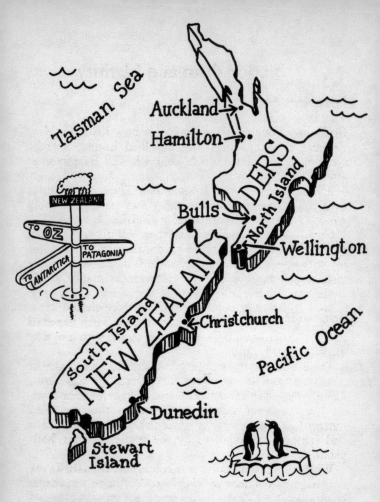

The Kiwi population is approaching 3¾ million (compared with 5 million Scots; 7 million Swiss; 18 million Aussies; 48 million English, and 256 million Americans).

New Zealand is six times bigger than Switzerland but could fit into Australia 28 times.

Nationalism and Identity

Forewarned

God's own country – 'Godzone' – is how Kiwis see New Zealand. Their picture is of unsullied beauty, friendly welcomes, fair play for one and all, and happily ever afters.

It isn't quite like that. It never was. These days there is even the suspicion that something may have gone sadly wrong, but at bottom the belief in Godzone is staunch.

Give Kiwis half a chance and they will prove it to you, stifling their own doubts the while. They will even come up with some slight imperfections. But heaven help the visitors who begin to criticise Godzone, especially if they come from the original European seedbeds – England, Scotland, Wales or Ireland – and therefore should know better. Only the Aussie visitor can criticise. He is expected to do so. There would be something wrong with him if he did not.

The Kiwis know theirs is the world's most spectacular scenery, the most varied and accessible, the most truly memorable. They cannot get enough praise of their country but they also mistrust it. They fear they are being buttered up. Somebody is having them on. Both praise and criticism are reported by the media, and are hotly debated.

When the English critic and columnist, Bernard Levin, devoted two columns in *The Times* to the incomparable beauties of New Zealand, this could not go unchallenged. During prime news time on New Zealand's biggest television channel the reporter telephoned Levin and quoted to him things like "loveliest country in the world?" Levin: "Yes, yes." "But do you really mean it?" Levin: "Of course." "Yes, but really..?"

5

Travellers must therefore tread a delicate course, at first rationing their praise to allow the beaming Kiwi to demur, but then coming back with a stronger counterpoint.

How Others See Them

'Friendly' is the adjective which crops up most in visitors' answers to surveys about how others see the Kiwis. Except for the Aussies, that is. The Aussies see them as a bit stodgy, backward because they produce only a few television soap operas, and generally behind the times. They are also an irritant, often popping up and winning which they have no right to do.

Kiwis are seen a lot overseas – because of their passion for travel it is a wonder there are any left in New Zealand – and are usually sought after, whether as team leaders, nannies or for any other job requiring versatility, stamina and resilience. Kiwis have to be versatile. There aren't enough of them for there to be specialists.

How Kiwis Would Like to be Seen

New Zealanders know they take rather more interest in other countries than other countries take in them. This grieves them a little, although they say politely that it's a natural consequence of being few in number, and living at the bottom of the map.

Kiwis enjoy letting the words 'Southern Hemisphere' roll off their lips. If something is the biggest, fastest or best 'in the Southern Hemisphere', it sounds much more important than just 'the biggest in New Zealand'.

A common preoccupation of Kiwis abroad is watching out for and counting the number of times the name of their country appears in their host country's newspapers. Twice in three months is considered good-going, even if the first mention may be news of an earthquake or a volcanic eruption, and the second is on the sports page. They also observe that New Zealand is where novelists send characters they don't know what to do with.

There are four names that Kiwis feel are reasonably well-known abroad: mountaineer Edmund Hillary, writer Katherine Mansfield, nuclear scientist Ernest Rutherford, and opera singer Kiri Te Kanawa. They think this is an absurdly short list in view of New Zealand's overall contribution to the world. As proof, they point to a household poll organised by New Zealand Post, the aim of which was to discover the most famous Kiwis in each of several categories. Those with most votes would be featured in a new stamp series. In the sports category alone there were 83 Kiwi contenders. That there were only a meagre 18 in the section for community leaders and social campaigners (in a country renowned for social crusading), may be simply because the pollsters, all true Kiwis, knew a lot about sports people but little about anybody else.

New Zealanders would like to be seen as people of consequence living in a country with much to offer, an oasis of beauty, and as a first step they wish the rest of the world would learn just where they are on the globe, and colour it clean green.

They would prefer to believe that the world's ignorance of many matters Kiwi is merely due to the fact that other countries have not achieved the Kiwis' degree of cosmopolitanism, but they suspect that, one way or another, it may be because they still do not count.

7

Special Relationships

For years the Kiwis suffered from reverse paranoia, the conviction that everyone who counted was out to be nice to them. This did not surprise them. They knew that deep down they were good keen men and women, lovable even.

Their strongest bond was with Britain, the Mother Country, the Old Country, Home – always with capital letters. Britain was simply taken for granted. After all, who questions the relationship with a dearly loved mother?

Kiwis were more patriotic than the British. What other country would set up a Coronation Rejoicing Committee? In trade, in attitudes, in peace and in war, they were as one, such as when their prime minister declared, at the outbreak of World War II, "Where Britain goes, we go." The trumpets sounded. There were no second thoughts.

Then in 1973, the unthinkable happened. Britain entered the EEC. Kiwis travelling to the Mother Country had to join the Heathrow queues marked 'Aliens'. This made the queues unmanageably long – there are more passports in New Zealand for each million people than there are in any other country in the world. Kiwis felt cast out from the bosom of their mother. They also discovered that she was no longer giving priority to their burgeoning exports of butter, meat, wool and kiwifruit.

By and large they still love Britain best. But signs of republicanism are breaking through. It isn't easy, coping with unrequited love.

A special relationship with the Americans grew up in World War II when New Zealand was used by thousands of marines as a training and staging post for the war in the Pacific. Families developed close ties with 'their' marine, and the huge casualty lists were deeply mourned.

The American invasion had a lasting influence on male-female relationships.

Because New Zealanders feel so close to the Americans, they were shocked by the angry alarm with which the US government reacted to the Kiwi nuclear-free policy of the 1980s, which prevents access of American nuclear-powered naval vessels to New Zealand territorial waters.

The mighty USA took it as an insult and a snub. As long as this little country was defiant, they declared, it would be cast out of the three-power ANZUS Treaty, the linchpin of Kiwi defence.

Like an unpopular child in the playground, New Zealand was left out while the United States and Australia (which exports uranium) played their war games and manoeuvres and whispered their military secrets to each other.

There's no fun when friends fall out, but relationships have noticeably improved since the lifting of the Iron Curtain. Americans visit in large numbers. Kiwis like them, and not just because of their pop music and movies. They took heart from the fact that not all Americans sided with their government during the tensest days of the nuclear disagreement. A popular bumper sticker in the US, frequently photographed and sent to friends in New Zealand, read, 'Wish I Were a Kiwi Nuclear-Free'.

The French enormously strengthened the Kiwi anti-nuclear stand by resuming their nuclear testing at Mururoa Atoll. Incensed that nuclear weapons should be tested in their Pacific backyard, Kiwis, backed by Aussies, led the united South Pacific opposition. Kiwis are not an especially religious people, but the Americans and French between them have brought about an almost religious conversion of the entire country to the anti-nuclear banner.

But it is Australians with whom Kiwis have the closest relationship. Kiwis head the list of visitors to Australia, and Aussies make up the largest single group to visit New Zealand. There is a great deal of trade and intermarriage and crossings of the Tasman Sea in both directions for study and work.

Periodic suggestions that New Zealand become the eighth state of Australia are fodder for cartoonists and derisive pub talk. Kiwis like to think that they can take on the Aussies at almost anything, so if you can lick them, why join them?

Whenever the Aussies show a distressing tendency to beat them at sport, Kiwis consider it a blip in the system, an aberration in the natural order of things. New Zealand horses always win the Melbourne Cup. If they don't, they should. New Zealand yachts beat the Aussies' yachts. The All Blacks won the first Rugby World Cup. The fact that the Aussies won the second resulted in a shrug (after passions had died down) and an "Ah well, next time". Kiwis know that when Aussies win, it's only because they have four or five times as many people to draw upon.

The Asian Connection

Although Singapore and Hong Kong are popular holiday destinations for Kiwis, they prefer to seek their Asian experience themselves rather than have it thrust upon them. In search of new markets, the government has worked at telling the nation they are part of the Pacific, part of Asia. To foster this belief, wealthy Asian immigrants have been invited in, with Auckland their first choice as base. They were supposed to bring investment capital with them, but it is suspected many come mainly to give their children a good education on the cheap.

This specially-favoured immigration of the wealthy was so ineptly handled by the government that it triggered racist reaction which ballooned into the political arena. Kiwis, who like to think they haven't a racist thought in their heads, suddenly discovered some heads had. Thus in Auckland, though not yet in the rest of the country, everyone knows the answer to this riddle:

Q: Your home has been burgled. How do you know the burglar is Asian?
A: If the cat's gone and the homework's been done.

A bonus to this riddle is that, as everyone also knows, Asians commit less crime than any other ethnic group. Give them a few generations in their new country and they'll learn.

How They See One Another

Kiwis do not need Aussies with their sheep jokes to remind them that New Zealand has far more sheep than it has people. There are some 50 million of them, and they graze almost everywhere. (Kiwis know Australia has many more sheep, but say they are much less in evidence because they have the good sense to graze far away from the cities so that they don't have to look at the Aussies.)

The people population is some 3.6 million, nearly three-quarters of whom live in the five main centres, one of which considers itself to be the only one that counts. In fact, it could be said that there are two geographic and psychic identities in New Zealand – Auckland, and the rest of the country.

Kiwis agree that Auckland is undoubtedly the biggest city. After that, opinions depend on where one lives:

11

Auckland is either brash, loud, self-centred, and quick to pick up foolish overseas fads; or it is exciting, innovative, the country's natural leader and the city with the best climate. Auckland forgets its feeling of superiority only when New Zealand as a whole is criticised.

As most white-skinned Kiwis, or *Pakeha* (Maori for non-Maori, or other), are descended from United Kingdom stock, telephone directories contain predominantly old English names together with pages of O', Mc, and Mac.

A good 13% of the population is Maori, but the directories do not give much indication of the fact. This is because there are no pure-blooded Maori left, and intermarriage has given half of them old English names and names beginning with O', Mc and Mac.

Most Kiwis see themselves as one people with two main cultures. Unlike Australians who opened their doors post-war to East Europeans, more Europeans, and then Vietnamese refugees, the Kiwis were suspicious of such new stock. They did accept Pacific peoples from closer to home – who now make up 5% of the population – but on the whole they took xenophobic pride in remaining true to the United Kingdom as their preferred source of new citizens, if new citizens they must have. Because of unemployment, new arrivals are not always given a wholehearted welcome – that is, if they come intending to stay.

The country's large number of Maori look with suspicion at the influx of Pacific Island peoples who come seeking jobs so they can help support their families back home. There are more Niueans and Cook Islanders in Auckland than there are in Niue or the Cooks, and the same will soon be true of other islands. One can thus get a Pacific Islands experience without actually having to go there.

Character

Kiwis are still so close to the official beginning of their country in 1840 that their character has grown directly out of the dangers, privations and challenges of pioneering. They remain doers rather than dreamers, even if most of the doing these days is done within the confines of the suburban quarter-acre.

Pioneering Spirit

Most of New Zealand was covered with dense bush when the European pioneers arrived. A pioneering Kiwi 'joker' (a.k.a. a bloke, mate, or chap) soon learned that pioneers didn't cry. Grin and bear it was the motto (but grumble all you like). They soon became dab hands at cutting down or burning trees, hurtling up and down mountains, and leapfrogging rivers. They had to, to get anywhere.

This pioneering spirit became known as Giving It a Go, whether or not you felt capable or had ever done it before.

Hostess at party to newcomer: "Can you play the piano?"
Guest: "No, but I'll give it a go."

The pioneering spirit and challenges go together. One dull day in 1986 a Kiwi named A. J. Hackett decided to throw himself from the Eiffel Tower. He called this bungee jumping. His company can now claim to have sent thousands of innocents hurtling earthwards from bridges or cantilevered platforms in many parts of the world, the only thing between them and the next world being a stout rubber cord (made of the same stuff as condoms, and approved by New Zealand Safety Standards) secured to their ankles.

13

Against all the evidence Kiwis persist in thinking they are more 'outdoorsy' than they really are. Man Against the Elements is a favourite entertainment theme, especially if it is something that can be watched on television in the comfort of your own home.

DIY

The Kiwis grow up expecting they'll do it themselves. "Piece of cake," they say. The population is spread so thinly over the islands that there are simply not enough tradesmen to go round. Besides, there is nothing like the triumph of fixing, enlarging, remodelling, and building from scratch.

Visitors are taken on tours of inspection, both inside the home and out. Hardware stores and garden centres do booming business at weekends when Kiwis, recuperating from a week's work, hurl themselves into the frantic activity of DIY.

Gardening is high on the list of traditional weekend occupations. It, too, is often tackled headlong so that the utmost can be wrung out of every spare moment. Gardens used to be divided strictly on gender lines. He did the vegetables, she the flowers. The women's movement counts among its significant gains the fact that most gardens are now unisex.

Towns and suburbs have garden competitions, and flower shows great and small are regular proof that almost anything grows bigger and better in New Zealand. Disbelievers are directed to study the hills of golden gorse and broom, importees from England which flourish so well in the benign climate that they have been declared noxious weeds.

For men, work on the car is its own reward. Many

vehicles are so old they look like escapees from a vintage car museum. It is not just sentiment which makes people regard their old cars as others do their faithful horses put out to grass. It is a Kiwi tradition to cannibalise parts, and keep cars going years past their normal use-by date. Canny Kiwis improvise and cajole a longer working life out of their cars than virtually any other nation.

For women, DIY extends to catering. The words 'Ladies a plate', as part of the notice of a function, have a long tradition. Catering is usually a shared enterprise, especially in rural areas, with women competing to bring along plates bearing the most impressive fare. Stories abound of newcomers to the country who arrive at a social function with half a dozen plates tucked under their arms, in the belief that the organisers are short of crockery.

Feminists can object as much as they like to the fact that only women are asked to contribute the food but it is the women who bake the cakes for that perennial small town fundraiser, the cake stall.

The great Kiwi cake is the eight-inches-high sponge sandwich, feather-light, dusted with icing sugar and joined together with raspberry jam and dollops of thick sweetened cream. The Heart Foundation just has to look the other way.

The Fair Go Concept

New Zealand was one of the first countries to establish an office of Race Relations Conciliator. This officer goes in for explanations to the majority of how the various minorities feel when they and their perceived customs are at the receiving end of jokes. Kiwis approve of this. They are wedded to the Fair Go principle, but they also like to laugh. The result is that the Race Relations Conciliator

15

has driven much humour underground, where it flourishes, usually affectionately, but with a cutting edge if imposed political correctness is involved. Kiwis do not like to be told how to think.

It is no accident that a television consumer programme is called *Fair Go*. It has been top-rated since it began in 1977, waging war against scams, cons and bureaucracy.

Kiwis place fair dealing and social justice at the top of the ladder of virtues – even when dealing with Aussies. After all, every kindergarten child knows this riddle:

Q: How can you tell an Aussie?
A: You can't tell an Aussie anything.

The Aussies are not considered the world's best sports, so are seen as fair game for taunting and teasing, especially with references to underarm bowling. This relates to the infamous occasion when, with one ball remaining in a cricket test in which New Zealand had one last crucial chance to win or at least even the score, an Aussie bowled underarm.

Fair's fair; which is why, although they enjoyed the joke at the time, they did not altogether approve of the tactics of the Kiwi advertising copywriter who, to push one of New Zealand's beers on the Australian market, capitalised on the fate of the Aussie yacht which was racing in the America's Cup when it suddenly broke in half and sank. The snappy caption to a full-page advertisement for the New Zealand beer declared, 'There's only one thing that goes down faster than an Aussie yacht'. Kiwis laughed, and then helped their rivals equip another yacht.

Funny yes. But not a Fair Go.

Behaviour

Understatement

Kiwis tend to deprecate that which they value most. "Not bad, eh", said of an achievement, is the very essence of pride. To show off, or 'skite', is to invite universal mockery and condemnation. To say of someone, "He likes the sound of his own voice", is to damn indeed.

A good Kiwi bloke plays things down and does not stand on ceremony. Someone who has scored a try at rugby is still expected to look as if he is bravely accepting a death sentence. Emotion is not something to be shown in public, and not much in private either (which may explain why such commercial inventions as Valentine's Day have been slow to take off). A blokess is allowed more latitude. She is even expected by men to 'carry on a bit'.

Television interviewers can have a hard time whipping up any semblance of emotion. A fireman emerging, blackened, from an inferno with a rescued child in his arms might allow to the camera that it was "a bit hot in there". If two cars are nearly demolished in a collision and the two drivers are able to limp away, one might say to the other, "That was close".

The Chopping Down Reflex

A Kiwi works on the premise that if it's taller than you are, chop it down. This applied to the original bush which covered the land and dwarfed the new settlers. So successful were they that huge areas became denuded and are now having to be re-clothed in man-made forest.

Kiwis feel that those who may think themselves superior, especially if they return home trailing clouds of glory acquired overseas, are asking to be chopped down to everyone else's level.

An exception to this rule is Sir Edmund Hillary. When he and Sherpa Tensing were the first to climb Mount Everest and there was all that fuss, the knives could have been readied back home. But Hillary showed he was just a good average Kiwi simply ticking something off his list of things to do, as it were, when he said, "We knocked the bastard off". Everyone could go along with that.

Manners

Kiwis expect and value what they call 'decent' behaviour. Conformity is king in small towns. Mild eccentricity sticks out and is therefore embarrassing. Full-blown eccentricity, on the other hand, may be worked up into a tourist attraction, such as the soothsaying, crowd-pulling and self-appointed Wizard of Christchurch, resplendent in wizardly robes.

Until not so very long ago the correct behaviour for a lady was to wear hat and gloves in public and not draw attention to herself. Now only the gloves remain for winter warmth.

Kiwi women are still close enough to pioneering life (or its traditions) to know that, in theory, 'girls can do anything' – and do. The legal issue of sexual harassment has caught a few males unaware. As a group, they have never shown the same degree of casual familiarity with women as have most Europeans, and what little did exist is slowly disappearing: whittled away, say some males, by a small but vociferous group of feminist police; banished at last, say these females, because of a new sexual maturity.

A popular wall decoration in those offices which are predominantly young and female says, 'Sexual harassment is not reported here, but is graded, one to ten'.

Politeness

Informality is the trademark of the Kiwi. Standing on ceremony is greeted with raised eyebrows. Anything that is seen as fussy, stuffy or over-elaborate is despised.

Yet politeness is valued and expected at all ages and stages. This is because there are so few people in New Zealand that everyone knows everyone else, or is related to, or at least a neighbour of, someone you might know. Speed of communication means that any lapse in manners is bound to be 'sheeted' home, so it swiftly becomes known. Too right.

Kiwis can carry politeness to considerable lengths. Someone who has been served with a cup of coffee may say to a waitress, "Excuse me, sorry, but may I have a teaspoon please?" If this were the US, the startled waitress would ask, "Where you from, honey?" In New Zealand she would say, "Sure, sorry, here you go". It is understood that the customer is not going anywhere, but just wanting to stir his coffee.

'Sorry' is the universal shorthand, the coinage of good manners, said by both people if they bump into each other in the street.

People working in businesses and services which are involved in tourism are strongly urged to enrol in the KiwiHost course, an imaginative but practical workshop with an emphasis on friendly hospitality, understanding visitors' needs, and general helpfulness. To Kiwis politeness is synonymous with warmth and generosity of spirit. Thus North Islanders, when complimented by visitors on their scenery, usually ask anxiously, "But have you seen the South Island yet?" They do not want to be seen as hogging the best bits for themselves.

'Bloody', the great Australian expletive, is frequently used, but not often in public places. Big hoardings in Australia do not mince their words when it comes to important messages. In Victoria, for instance, a safe driving campaign was highly successful when roadsides bloomed with exhortations 10 feet high: 'If you drink and drive you're a bloody fool.' Greatly daring, Kiwi road safety authorities borrowed the idea and now speak, still comparatively mildly, of 'bloody idiots'.

Even Parliament, once the home of the robust denunciation and few-holds-barred debate, has become almost polite, which may explain why politicians are considered so boring. An old-time Labour MP was once accused of profiteering and acquiring great holdings in timber. He jumped to his feet and declared that he "didn't own enough timber to build a shithouse for a cockroach". Nowadays nobody in public life would dream of saying 'shithouse'.

As a rule, four-letter words are frowned on, no matter how ancient their Anglo-Saxon lineage (unless the occasion is an all-male gathering, or stag night). Kiwis are firm about using genteel language in print or in mixed company. Four-letter words are tackled this way:

A scribe, to the vulgar inclined,
Wrote a play more gross than refined,
With words, all four-letter
Hips, nips, tits and better
Like those that have just crossed your mind.

Conversation

Kiwis feel awkward if they sit or stand next to someone for any length of time and do not talk. This is a brazen reversal of the British habit of keeping oneself to oneself and can be blamed on the very newness of New Zealand. There were so few people in the country for so many years that the first hardy types had to talk to themselves or they would forget how. Their excitement when they encountered another human naturally caused them to utter – most probably "Gidday" or "How yuh doing?", the great Kiwi ice-breakers.

The most frequently used couple of words are 'you know', said with a rising inflection. Nobody is actually expected to know. It is just a useful filler while one is thinking of what to say next.

Standard topics of conversation between Kiwis flow smoothly and safely from and to the weather. Any change in the previous few days' weather pattern becomes that day's greetings. "Hot enough for you?" or "Cold enough for you?" The changes are rung with 'sunny enough', 'wet enough', and so forth.

Recent English immigrants are about the only people to say "Mustn't grumble" and then go right ahead and grumble. Everyone else just grumbles. Keeping up a stream of good-natured derision directed at politicians, weather forecasters, the economy, and anyone getting too big for his breeches is the custom of the country.

Another is the continuous lip-service to optimism: whether or not there is a need to worry about something, the obliging Kiwis tell one another that it will be 'good as gold', 'right as rain' and 'no prob' (short for problem), usually qualified by one of those great reassurers in any situation, 'She'll be right', or 'Piece of cake'.

Kiwis encountered when you are at the beach, in the

street or sharing public transport, like to be asked for advice: it gives them the chance to be friendly and helpful. The farther south you go, the friendlier the people. Maybe it's because they are lonelier. Those people waving from a roadside on the remote West Coast, for instance, are unlikely to be flagging you down for help. They are just enjoying a moment of contact.

Attitudes and Values

The Treaty of Waitangi

New Zealand has long regarded itself as a racial paradise. It certainly seemed that way to the Pakeha. There was equality for everyone under the law, work for everyone who wanted it, and the state provided social security so that nobody lived in poverty. The only barrier to a Maori becoming successful in a chosen career seemed to be a lack of confidence.

But this is far too simplistic a view and is based on ignorance of history and of Maori culture. The Maori has been particularly hard hit by the government's belt-tightening and resulting unemployment. Old grievances which have simmered for generations have begun boiling to the surface. Throughout the media and almost anywhere you go, the Treaty of Waitangi is under discussion. This treaty was signed on 6 February 1840 between the British Crown and Maori chiefs, the Maori having arrived from their mythical Hawaiki some 600-800 years earlier (tribal versions vary on this point).

The treaty gave the Maori sovereignty over their natural resources. Just what this means is being earnestly debated, which is a polite way of saying that the extremists on both sides are increasingly frustrated, and vocal.

There are genuine injustices. Land was not always bought fairly and squarely, either intentionally or through misunderstanding of multiple Maori ownership. Sometimes it was simply taken. The law, in the shape of the Waitangi Tribunal, deals very slowly with land claims. It is underfunded (many would say deliberately), so does not have the resources to move quickly; and besides, at the end of the day, it merely makes recommendations.

Even though Maori have equal rights and responsibilities under the law (without necessarily feeling that all the responsibilities apply to them), they do not feel the law takes into account their almost mystical relationship with the land. This relationship is talked about more now that some 70% have left their rural bases, or *marae*, for the towns, where many have still not found fulfilment.

To make matters more difficult, Maori tribes do not agree about how to tackle their grievances. Tribes have a long history of disagreement. In fact, they may have been the ultimate xenophobes. To them the tribe next door were strangers. They did not only fight them. They ate them.

Many of the young, especially if they lack skills or jobs, want revolutionary change. Television is their ally – "If it protests, shoot it" is the instruction to all cameramen, so protesters are guaranteed their moment of televisual fame.

But inter-tribal rivalries and differences still prevent them from speaking with one voice. The rest of the country wishes they would just join forces and get on with it, but this is not the Maori way. A key part of Maori language and culture is the *hui* or get-together within a tribe, where oratory explores every possible issue, sometimes for days on end. It is not a method entirely suited to a digit-ticking, technological age.

The Kiwi Class System

Kiwi society is composed of three main groups and a self-labelled elite, all with strong feelings about the way they see themselves.

Sensitive New Age Kiwis (SNAKS) are found in urban areas and in life-style blocks on the outskirts of towns. Traditional Old-fashioned Rural Kiwis (TORKS) are out in the rest of the country. Among them are 'rednecks' – ultra-conservative small farm holders, and almost equally conservative businesspeople determined to keep what they've got – who usually form the majority in Parliament and on local bodies. The Maori, particularly the younger generation, are increasingly seen as Independently Willed Indigenous Kiwis (IWIKS).

Class distinctions are based more on education than on money or belonging to old families. Better Educated New Zealanders (BENZERS) regard themselves as the elite and look down on most SNAKS (as being foolishly trendy), nearly all TORKS (for obvious reasons), and some but by no means all IWIKS.

BENZERS are a minority. Asians are correct when they perceive that Kiwis do not place education high in the scheme of things. BENZERS would never dream of calling themselves, or others, Kiwis. They regard the word merely as a vulgar device to fit the label New Zealanders into a headline. In this attitude they are hopelessly in the minority. Female BENZERS, in particular, are convinced they have much to offer the rest of the world, this conviction dating from 1893 when New Zealand became the first country where women had the vote.

Some TORKS have aspirations to become SNAKS, whereas some SNAKS are reverting to type and becoming TORKS when confronted by the demands of radical IWIKS. An IWIK can also be a SNAK, TORK or BENZER.

TORKS like to see themselves as the rightful contenders in the struggle to secure the world's main agricultural markets although, as farms amalgamate and become more mechanised, there are far fewer farmers than there used to be. SNAKS, with some extra-sensitive reservations about the growing gap between the haves and have-nots, consider they are part of the global community, leading it in terms of economic and societal growth. IWIKS see themselves as a sovereign people, with all the rights but not quite all the obligations of other Kiwis. BENZERS believe the other groupings would see the light if only they were better educated. None of these views is realistic.

The one thing they have in common is that they all regard themselves as rugged pioneers capable of fixing anything with a piece of number eight fencing wire (the country's staple tool since pioneering days), and perfectly able, most of the time, to take on the rest of the world at anything, particularly sport.

Family Life

Strongly-bonded family loyalty is seen as the backbone of society, hence the sympathy with the Queen in her domestic problems. Regard for family life remains even though the nature of the family has changed, with the concept both enlarging and shrinking. Maori and Pacific Island peoples, with their tradition of the big extended family, have pointed one way, and the many single-parent households, mostly headed by women, the other.

The marriage rate for the entire country is going down year by year, and the average age for a first marriage has risen to 30 for women and 33 for men. De facto relationships and solo parenthood increase. However, romance is far from dead; daughters still plan a traditional white (or off-white) wedding, with bridesmaids, reception and honeymoon – the full whack.

The divorce rate is high. A period of two years of formal separation is grounds for divorce, with no need for the peccadilloes of either partner to be hauled through the courts and the media.

A high proportion of children come from homes with just one parent. It is relatively common among Maori and Polynesians for children to be looked after solely by a grandparent or other older guardian. This may have worked well in the former, highly-organised, tribal societies but, with most Maori now living away from their tribal bases, in towns and cities, it is hard for grandparents in isolation to catch up on and cope with all the changes which children accept as a matter of course.

At the other end of life, granny flats are popular but most elderly people prefer living alone independently while they can. A growth industry is the rest home, the 'Peacehavens', where the frail elderly can go, some by choice in order not to be a burden on their families, others because they have nobody willing or able to look after them. Maori and Pacific Island peoples are conspicuously absent from this last group. Honouring the aged is part of their culture.

European settlers were mainly Protestant, and Protestant values still hold sway although not necessarily to the extent of actual attendance in church. Most people, when asked to name their religion, will say Church of England (Anglican), then Presbyterian, Roman Catholic or Methodist, the faiths of their founding fathers.

Methodism is strong among many Pacific Island groups. The Church of the Latter Day Saints (Mormons) and Jehovah's Witnesses claim many Maori adherents. Faith is often a matter of which missionary got there first.

Obsessions

The Weather

The weather is the Kiwi's number one obsession.

Because New Zealand is a long skinny country of three main islands, nobody lives far from the sea. New Zealand sits plunk in the middle of the ocean and thousands of kilometres from any other substantial land mass. This explains its unique vegetation and wild life but is also why it is so hard for meteorologists to predict what kind of weather is going to reach what part of the country. Bad weather, of course, always comes over the Tasman Sea from Australia.

The media cash in on this preoccupation by trying to make personalities out of the forecasters (in a country which feels itself short of recognisable characters). The forecasters themselves, when saying that the weather will be fine, have taken to hedging their bets. They will say, for instance, that there's a 15% chance they'll be wrong.

Students of journalism are given special tuition in handling weather stories and the ramifications, social and economic, of long stretches of either drought or storm.

There is one constant. The nation's farmers are never satisfied with what they get and even less satisfied with the forewarnings. They never believe them, anyway.

Since everyone is affected by the dramatic weather changes when planning work or leisure activities (a torrential downpour for five solid hours can make a difference to your day), in many households the peak hour radio and television forecasts are listened to with almost religious intensity. It is not done to telephone people at such times.

Sport

Running the weather a close second in the obsession stakes is sport in all its manifestations. The All Blacks are deified, and champions of lesser sports idolised. The match of the day, the day of the match, the player of the day, the week, the year – in every conceivable sport the drums of publicity beat for ever more heroes.

There are still not so many recognised heroines. In spite of the fact that in the all-female sport of netball they have been world champions, it is taking women a while to get public recognition. But when Susan Devoy, the Kiwi who for years was the women's squash champion of the world, gave up competing and had a baby, companies fell over themselves to get her endorsement for their products.

Role models for the young come almost exclusively from the sporting arena and increasingly include Maori and Pacific Island peoples. Whenever there is a well-publicised world contest and the Kiwis are likely to win, everyone, male or female, young or old, settles in rapt concentration round their radio and television sets.

Politics

Another obsession is with politics and politicians. Kiwis like to think they are politically well informed. They are fed a constant stream of political news, anecdotes and personality pieces, more than enough to fuel incessant discussion and controversy.

Any political scandal looms large because there is a (perhaps) surprising degree of probity among elected representatives. In Australia politicians are routinely called scumbags, quite often with cause. In New Zealand the worst thing that can be said about many of them is that they are boring.

The whole country laughed when two senior and avowedly redneck government politicians were caught in a joke which misfired. One, the Minister of Tourism, was running a weekly radio talkback show not noted for its sensitivity. A journalist recognised the voice of a caller who said his name was Hone (Maori for John) and that he was unemployed; he carried on, using an exaggerated Maori intonation, to make plain he wasn't interested in finding a job as life was much easier on the dole. The journalist exposed the caller as none other than the friend and colleague of the Minister of Tourism – the Senior Government Whip.

Kiwi politicians have no tradition of honourable resignation. They don't go unless they are pushed. The Senior Government Whip, alias Hone, was pushed, and he resigned his post (though remaining an MP) as a direct result of the public uproar. The majority clearly agreed that the Maori should not be insulted in this way – while continuing to chuckle.

Kiwis have always believed in having a bet both ways.

Animals

As the nation's economy was built on farm animals, it is not surprising that animal welfare is high on the list of Kiwi concerns. Under a new law which allows a referendum to be held when enough signatures to a petition have been gathered, one of the first crusades was to ban the practice of rearing battery hens. Parliament, however, had carefully framed the legislation so that it was not bound to pass any result into law. Everyone knew this, but signed the petition all the same, to let parliament know how they felt.

Horses are the number one favourite animal. If it were not so hard to keep them in a quarter-acre section, they might even outnumber the nation's cats and dogs (though not, of course, the sheep). Children beg to belong to pony clubs and Kiwi riders such as Mark Todd often carry off the trophies at international horse events.

But the best place for a horse is on the race course and first past the post. It's not for nothing that 'you bet' is Kiwi for a very firm 'yes'. The TAB (Totalisator Agency Board, or betting shop) is handily placed in every centre.

The passion for the horse helps bind New Zealanders to the British Royal Family.

Hunting and Pest Control

In its primal state New Zealand had practically no native animals except birds and seals. All other animals have been imported. Pests such as wasps have sneaked in, but there are no poisonous creatures except for a very rarely seen native spider, the katipo.

Hunting is an obsession, and a variety of species of deer was introduced for sport. They soon multiplied to the point where the government was forced to employ deer cullers, tough outback men who created their own mythology. The Department of Conservation, or DOC, wants to see the bush free from the ravages of deer. Not surprisingly, the Deer Stalkers Association and those with tourism interests see it differently. The Kiwis were propelled into deer farming with the discovery that some parts of the world would pay high prices for various parts of the deer, from the meat to the supposedly aphrodisiac velvet.

Two unfortunate animals have forfeited any claim to national sympathy and are obsessively hunted down. The rabbit which came from Britain and the possum from Australia gobble up pastures and native bush. The possum is also partial to orchard, rose and vegetable garden. Successive governments wax and wane in their support for possum and rabbit destruction programmes, with long-term hopes pinned on the discovery of birth control measures. One entrepreneur had the bright idea of giving possums the marketable name of 'Kiwi bears' and attempting to sell the meat – a not very exciting cross between chicken and rabbit. Few people have been fooled.

Furry corpses found on country roads are possums. Rabbits are too canny. The Kiwi who wants to clinch an argument with someone he regards as a naïve idealist propounding a hopeless cause will say, regardless of the topic, "You'll never catch the last rabbit".

Leisure and Pleasure

Sport is the Kiwi's main leisure interest. This means following broadcasts, going to watch, and taking part – in that order.

The main preoccupations of the male Kiwi have always been rugby, horse racing and beer. Rugby is still up there at the top though it is being challenged by other sports; race meetings are having to struggle for patrons in the face of newer betting opportunities; and beer is now actually being challenged by wine.

For most of New Zealand's history, rugby union has

been unquestionably the national sport. It is now in danger of being overshadowed by rugby league. The latter's top professional teams can afford extensive promotion to woo the public. Rugby union administrators (like their counterparts in Britain) struggle with the concept of professionalism to keep their game at the top and now pay their leading players. Sports writers analyse lucrative contracts as much as the actual games.

Only when the performance of Kiwi cricketers became so abysmal that watching them was no longer something to look forward to, did television viewers take to following the Aussie team instead, and that has to be the pits.

Yachting

Any parent can tell you that it's no surprise the Kiwis excel at yachting. Children can easily get to a lake or the sea and learn to sail a little Optimist dinghy, and it's better to have them out in a boat in all that healthy fresh air than underfoot at home when you are watching sport on television or getting on with your DIY.

Nothing has given the Kiwis as much pleasure as winning the world's premier yachting trophy. The whole country followed the 'best of nine' yacht races. The fact that New Zealand could play David to the American Goliath with all their space age resources was a great boost to national pride. And when Team New Zealand won the first five races in the final to beat the American holder of the America's Cup, joy and triumph reached record-breaking heights.

Half a million people (one seventh of the entire population) converged on the main cities on successive days to welcome the yachties home. Offices and schools closed, ticker tape and balloons filled the air, and strong Kiwis dashed tears from their eyes. It was as if the whole country had just won the national lottery. "You played fair," said the welcoming Governor-General, and others declared it was just like conquering Everest all over again.

Arts and Leisure Festivals

A rapidly spreading event in many parts of New Zealand is the annual learning festival with workshops in the arts and activities such as sailing and kayaking. These have grown out of the new economic emphasis on helping yourself and not looking to the state to save you. You can learn to paint, sail a yacht or write a novel, all for a ridiculously small sum of money – especially if your novel becomes a bestseller.

Even small towns are capitalising on their local attractions, artists and leisure leaders. Highly individual and well-patronised festivals result, bringing a boost to local economies. Bulls, a junction township named after a pioneer settler, decided it might as well capitalise on all the jokes about its name. Virtually all its businesses have renamed themselves. A café is Delect-a-bull, an antiques and souvenir business is Collect-a-bull. Need a money machine? Go to the banks' Cash-a-bull. Firemen are Extinguish-a-bulls and cops, Const-a-bulls. The public loos are Relieve-a-bulls, and if people feel they need absolution they can go to the local church, Forgive-a-bull. The citizens are waiting for their population to justify a family planning clinic. It would of course be Inconceive-a-bull.

Other places have promoted new sports such as gumboot throwing and kiwifruit throwing to give themselves a distinctive character. Throughout the country, organising and self-betterment committees thrive. They have a long history. A group of early settlers, stumped for something exciting to do in their rare leisure time, formed themselves into an Egg-Laying Competition Committee.

Sense of Humour

Kiwis like laughing, particularly at politicians and any others silly enough to set themselves up as knowing what's best for everyone else.

They enjoy outwitting bureaucrats. A winemaker just south of the little town of Picton, near where the main wine-producing country begins, wanted to excavate a hillside behind his premises, to make a wine cellar. He was refused a building permit. He gave the matter some thought, applied instead for a mining permit, and now big wooden doors set in the hillside lead connoisseurs and tourists into his 'wine mine'.

Much of the humour is home-grown. Pakeha and Maori used to make good-humoured jokes about each other, but the imported doctrine of political correctness has had an inhibiting effect. These days people are inclined to tiptoe around, afraid of giving offence. They long for another Billy T. James, the late comedian who genially made fun of Maori and Pakeha alike, and had everyone laughing. Billy thrived on sending up race relations, treaty issues and tribal rivalries. When a radical Maori woman said, "Kill a white and be a hero!", Billy said plaintively, "What about all us halfcastes? Do we just get wounded or something?" And he said of himself: "I'm half Maori and half Scots. Half of me wants to go to the pub and get pissed, and the other half doesn't want to pay for it."

On the whole it is safer and equally traditional to make Aussies the butt of jokes. For example:

The Aussies have just discovered a new use for sheep. Wool.

Have you heard about the new fast film they've brought out? It's so fast you can actually take a picture of an Aussie with his mouth shut.

Another comedian, John Clark, who has gone so far as to exile himself to Australia, returns periodically to give Kiwis the lowdown on doings trans-Tasman. He dresses for television in black singlet and gumboots, and his yarns are country-style leisurely and in accord with his stage name, which is Fred Dagg. Dags are those pieces of wool, manure-encrusted, which adorn the backside of a sheep. In the Kiwi system of inverted humour, it is something of a compliment to be called "a bit of a dag" − it means others are amused by your antics and admire you. And when Kiwis want someone to to hurry up and get a move on, they say, "C'mon! Rattle your dags!".

The Kiwis are quick to pounce. One Prime Minister, universally seen as somewhat pompous and plum-in-the-mouth, was rash enough to agree to address a student rally together with the Leader of the Opposition on whose side the students soon showed themselves to be. The Prime Minister was asked a question. He pondered, and then articulated slowly, "I — don't — think..." whereupon the whole audience roared as one, "You never think!"

Another Prime Minister, noted for his one-liners, was also facing students but this time in Oxford, debating America's foreign policy at an Oxford Union debate. When his American opponent duly trotted out the line that the nuclear bomb was essential to world peace, this

Kiwi brought the house down on his side by declaring, "I can smell the uranium on your breath."

Kiwis have a good line in gallows humour:

Novice to a betting man: "You good at picking winners?"

Betting man: "Dunno, I picked the Germans in the last two world wars."

Custom and Tradition

The Christmas holidays are the most important time for the family-centred Kiwis. 'Going home for Christmas' is the rule rather than the exception, and Christmas lasting to the end of January, when the children go back to school, is real holiday time for families.

It is not always as much a pleasure as a tradition when tents and sleeping bags and holiday gear are packed into cars along with the children and the pets, and the long drive begins, often from one end of the country to the other. Many people have their own favoured holiday spots, with 'baches' (originally bachelors' quarters of minimum comfort) by lakes, rivers, and sea.

Kiwis feel that just because these holidays fall in high summer is no reason for departing from the old English-style Christmas dinner of hot roast turkey and all the traditional accompaniments. Daring cooks try to change the menu to suit the temperature – but it's never the same.

Christmas and the month of January are not good times to visit New Zealand. Hardly anyone is at home. But travelling around New Zealand does not constitute 'travel' to a Kiwi. Real travel means going overseas (a flight of 20 hours or more), which is a serious business as well as a pleasure and has to be prepared for. Just going over the Tasman Sea to Australia, a three-hour journey, scarcely counts.

Middle-aged Kiwis who can afford it make the pilgrimage to the United Kingdom, Europe and Disneyland as soon as the children are off their hands. Able-bodied young Kiwis do their OE (overseas experience) before settling down to career and family. Often they choose Asia or the USA before, or even rather than, going to Britain. Sometimes they stay away. It is perfectly possible in Edinburgh, say, to meet a Maori with a broad Scots accent.

Neighbourliness

In small towns and in the country everyone knows everyone else's business. This is called being neighbourly. Even in the cities people know who their actual neighbours are, and are usually on visiting terms with them. Keeping in touch is a legacy from earliest pioneering days. You kept in touch or you perished.

A constant flow between town and country for visits and holidays accounts for much of New Zealand's traffic. Most Maori still feel strongly connected to their *marae* back in their tribal heartlands, and many non-Maori are nostalgic for their ancestors' country customs.

Never mind that architects point out how much heat is wasted when wood is burnt on an open fire. Those who can afford to revert to pioneering ways and have open fireplaces built into their new houses. Real flames flickering might not heat the whole house but they give it a heart, a welcoming centre.

The good housewife makes her own jams, sauces and chutneys just as her forebears did. She may freeze fruits and vegetables rather than preserve them in glass jars to place proudly on pantry shelves, but she is likely to have gathered at least some of the produce from her own garden. It's not done to question the extra cost in terms of time, effort and money.

Farm Rituals

Every shearing time the clear air becomes heavy with the hand lotion-lanolin smell of fresh creamy fleeces. Good shearers are national heroes, and all shearers must be fed well and at frequent intervals. The women of the farms tote baskets of home-cooked buttery scones, cream-filled sponges and heavy fruit cake to the shearing sheds every morning and afternoon 'smoko' time. Fewer shearers now smoke but this simply gives them more time for eating and disposing of gallons of strong tea which they drink in great sweetened gulps.

Smoko fare is just to keep them going between the three cooked meals each day. These begin with the traditional Kiwi farm breakfast of lamb chops, eggs, bacon and potato, the latter fried from the leftovers of the huge pot of the night before. Dieticians know it's hands off the shearers' tucker.

The sheepfarmers, or high country runholders, have been lords of the land almost since European settlement began, certainly since 1882 when refrigerated shipping made lamb exports possible. While governments paid out subsidies, they grew as fat as the lambs which rippled down the hillsides in white woolly tides.

These days sheep numbers are down by more than a

third since the mid-1980s. Cattle are making a comeback with the world's recognition that Kiwi beef comes from clean, green pastures. But the biggest demand is for the country's butter and cheese. Dairy farmers are better served by their marketing managers than are their much more conservative brethren of meat and wool production.

Farmers have a field-day grumbling. Their suspicion of the government – any government – is fuelled by what they see as economic manipulation. Subsidies for traditional farming have been swept away, yet there are big tax concessions for people who establish forests. This means that grazing land is being gobbled up by radiata pine. To make matters worse, the farmers say, these Johnny-come-latelies usually aren't farmers at all, just city slickers, paper-shufflers, jokers who have accountants to tell them how to make money. Meanwhile sombre pine trees march by the million over huge chunks of the landscape. At least they're green.

The sweeping pastures offer space, solitude and silence, except, that is, for the singing of the birds, and the mooing, and maa-ing and baa-ing of the livestock, and sheepdogs barking if it's mustering time, and the robust language of the musterers.

Kiwis accept that a flow of basic Anglo-Saxon – all those short, sharp words – is the only language a Kiwi sheepdog understands; that, and a few borrowings from the Bible. One reason for the great popularity of sheepdog trials on television is that viewers identify and sympathise with the plight of the contestants. When faced with a mob of contrary sheep to get through the hurdles, and no language suitable for public use, how on earth do you get your dog to obey commands? It's a national sport watching and waiting to see if man and beast can safely navigate these perils.

A Solemn Occasion

The year's most solemnly observed morning (the pubs are open in the afternoon) is Anzac Day, on 25th April.

The initials stand for Australia New Zealand Army Corps, and the day commemorates the Battle of Gallipoli on the Turkish peninsula on that day in 1915, during World War I. So many young men lost their lives then that the mingled grief and pride of both countries forms an enduring bond.

Anzac Day is when sacrifices in wars throughout the world are remembered, and hopes of world peace are given an airing. Even the smallest town has its war memorial. Young and old attend Anzac Day services from dawn, the former servicemen and women parading with medals, wreaths and deep solemnity. In the afternoon they talk, remember and drink.

What's Sold Where

New Zealand long retained many of its customs and traditions from the other side of the world and from the last century. Little was sold on a Saturday, and nothing on Sunday, causing Clement Freud (in a broadside widely reported of course) to say that he had visited New Zealand but that it was closed for the weekend.

'Saturday opening' was a hard-fought battle. Churches and trade unions maintained it would mean the end of family life if Mum had to serve behind a counter on Saturdays. Those who had travelled talked nostalgically of all-day shopping in more cosmopolitan societies, and most families said how nice it would be to be able to shop together, not to mention pleasing visitors. As usual, pragmatism and opportunism won the day.

Now it's 'open slather' (a free-for-all) in tourist centres every day of the week. Some businesses such as supermarkets, DIY stores and garden centres are introducing enthusiastic Kiwis to a new commercial age of all-day every-day shopping and in the rest of the country shops sell madly on Saturday mornings to make up for the lost years.

Even the smallest village has at least one 'dairy'. Dairies do indeed sell milk and butter but practically everything else as well. They are the country's convenience stores. Milk is still delivered to the door in glass bottles, but plastic and cardboard containers are increasingly used, and give rise to clamour about wasted resources and waste disposal.

Most service stations sell a week-long range of snacks and basic foods as well as car and handyman accessories, and even materials for home renovation. They know they'll always have a steady stream of customers ready to give it a go.

Kiwi Icons

Certain objects of everyday living are so dear to the Kiwi heart that the sight or even mention of them can bring on an instant attack of homesickness in the Kiwi abroad.

When the postal authorities decided to bring out an issue of stamps to celebrate Kiwiana, or the essence of being a Kiwi, it was not too hard to decide on ten significant items.

Four were foods, four were items of clothing, and two were things uniquely New Zealand.

Fish and chips, pavlova meringue dessert and kiwifruit were natural contenders. The fourth raised smiles of recognition round the country and overseas. There, triumphant on a postage stamp, was a mountainous cone of mouth-watering hokey pokey ice-cream, studded with glistening jewel-like chips of golden hokey pokey toffee which every Kiwi knows and loves.

Two items of working gear, plus one for sports and one for leisure, made up the clothing section of the stamp issue. One was the boldly-checked, heavy cotton bush shirt or swandri which is standard farm and forest wear (except in summer when it is usually a black singlet), and especially favoured by shearers. Gumboots (never called wellingtons) completed the working outfit.

Rugby boots stood for sports in general. Leisure was summed up by what Kiwis call 'jandals', the thick-soled, plastic, strap-between-the-toes, beach footwear which others call thongs or flip-flops.

Paua shell or abalone was an obvious choice. Most homes have paua shell items of some kind or other. When not used as ash trays or soap dishes, their gleaming, pearly, iridescent insides make exquisite jewellery, or souvenir-type trinkets, such as little shell animals with paua eyes.

Highly popular with the whole country was the stamp which showed a Buzzy Bee – an inspired, Kiwi-designed, pull-along toy for toddlers, with a bright red, low-slung body and wings and brilliant yellow and black face with antennae, which makes a most satisfactory noise when tugged. Kiwis loyal to the Crown do not expect the Royal Family to stock up with bushshirts and jandals, or even paua-shell ashtrays. But there was a great grin of pleasure when a photograph was published of Charles and Diana and their young sons. There, in the forefront of the family group, was the heir to the throne playing with a Kiwi Buzzy Bee.

Culture

New Zealand's national song is *God Defend New Zealand*, to which many people add, sotto voce, "Because nobody else will".

Add to this the best-known line from the best-known poet of earlier years, Thomas Bracken, "Not understood...", and you have some kind of insight into the shaky foundations of Kiwi culture.

For generations all eyes and ears were turned to Britain. Art critics have long accused Kiwis of the 'cultural cringe', of bowing down before anything British in preference to what comes out of New Zealand. British is both better and safer, goes the theory. Anything foreign is a bit threatening. Of course, anything American in this context does not count as foreign.

Television

New Zealand's primary source of culture is television. This means English and American drama series, entertainments and documentaries, with a handful of home-grown entries presented with a fanfare that is usually undeserved. There are also innumerable imported games shows, sports and more sports, news and backgrounders – all constantly interrupted by commercials on every channel.

The soaps prepare the young for life as they do in most western countries. One of New Zealand's three main TV channels has a highly popular local soap, *Shortland Street*. It is set in an Auckland inner-city clinic where love affairs, misgivings, mix-ups, unwanted pregnancies, misconceptions and occasional illness and accident are swiftly dealt with for 30 minutes (less commercial breaks) in prime time every week night. *Shortland Street* is now the main source of sex and family life education for the nation's teenagers. It shows that Maori, Polynesian and Pakeha are equally adept at seduction and being misunderstood.

Film

After years in the doldrums, Kiwi feature films suddenly figured at Cannes and on Oscar night. Three films in particular, all as different from one another as they could be, had Kiwis, as well as millions from the rest of the western world, rushing off to the cinema.

Singly or together, *The Piano*, *Once Were Warriors*, and *Heavenly Creatures* gave the world a rum view of New Zealand. Of course, not every New Zealand beach has a piano threatened by the waves; not every Maori gets drunk and beats his wife; and not many teenage girls plot with girlfriends to kill their mothers. But it has to be admitted that there is a taste for the serious, if not down-right depressing, in New Zealand's films, plays and fiction. But then Kiwis enjoy considering situations in the light of whether or not the protagonists have been given a Fair Go.

Music

The Maori opera singer, Kiri Te Kanawa, is the country's darling. On her occasional visits home, thousands who would never go to an opera throng her open-air concerts and get musically educated in spite of themselves.

When Maori perform at concerts, their beautiful harmony comes from the singing of European melodies, and the instruments are imported guitars. Authentic

Maori music does not appeal to the modern ear – nor, indeed, to the modern Maori.

Literature

The unofficial poet laureate, Allen Curnow, has had his poem *Landfall in Unknown Seas* set to music by the leading composer, Douglas Lilburn, and read by Sir Edmund Hillary. Its first lines open up the glorious possibilities of a new country, this New Zealand:

> Simply by sailing in a new direction
> You could enlarge the world.

And the stanza ends:

> On a fine morning, in the Name of God
> Into the nameless waters of the world.

It is this newness that is never far from the back of Kiwis' minds. It is part of the freshness and verve, the 'give anything a go', which is threaded through the national psyche. The poem is a bit highbrow for Kiwis to go round chanting in droves, but it expresses what many try to articulate.

Two poets, Sam Hunt and Gary McCormick, who barnstorm the country and take their poetry to the pubs, are equally at home out in the sticks. McCormick has founded what may be the country's most popular political movement, the Pull Yourself Together Party. In short weekly sessions on national radio, the Pull Yourself Together Party gives bracing rallying calls and instant solutions to the woes of the week.

Authentic voices from the new world have not had to be highbrow. Deer culling in the most remote reaches of the New Zealand bush produced book after book of the tallest tales by Barry Crump. The titles of his best-known are purest Kiwi: *A Good Keen Man*, and *Hang On a Minute, Mate*, are long, meandering, outback yarns which make the Kiwi laugh, even if he is sitting at his state-of-the-art computer.

It has been said of two of the most influential writers, Katherine Mansfield and Frank Sargeson, that they have afflicted New Zealand writing because many would-be authors have tried, but failed, to imitate their very different styles.

The country's heroes remain its sports people, not its artists, not Booker prize winner Keri Hulme with the sudden fame of her novel *the bone people,* not even someone as popular as detective story writer Ngaio Marsh. When the writer Janet Frame (*An Angel at My Table*) was being discussed as a possible winner of the Nobel Prize for Literature, nobody thought it necessary to prepare for crowds taking to the streets with ticker tape as they did for Team New Zealand when it brought home the America's Cup.

Tucker and Grog

New Zealand's climate, soils and waters mean that home-produced food, beer and wines are so good that it is difficult not to dine well.

It wasn't always so. The pre-European Maori had slim pickings. Almost the only foods were fish, birds, fern-roots and *kumara,* the delicious sweet potato. The biggest bird, biggest in the Southern Hemisphere, biggest in the world, was the giant moa, descended from pre-history. Changes in climate hastened its extinction, but the Maori fondness for sucking the marrow from the moa's long leg-bones didn't help. The kiwi, adopted as the national bird, was more elusive, and lucky in not being as tasty. Today's Kiwis think there's a moral there somewhere.

Maori placenames often commemorate food. *Kai* means food or a meal, and *koura* is crayfish, so the town of Kaikoura, base for watching whales and dolphins, means great tucker, or dining on the best.

As for grog, since the early 1980s the country has been transformed from a footnote in the catalogue of the world's wines into one of the leading chapters. The white wines in particular regularly win gold medals on the international stage. The toughest, bluffest Kiwi joker may hold forth on "a cheeky little sauvignon blanc with subtle, mouth-filling flavours with just a hint of fig, all combined with a clean, crisp finish".

Were it not for high government tariffs, wine might be as much part of mealtimes in every home as it is in France. Only 'might', because the Kiwi drink from pioneering days has been, and still is, beer. Beer is the great thirst-quencher, the great sporting drink, and still what 'the boys' rush into the pub and order.

In the far south, however, where the early settlers from Scotland put a lasting brand on the country, the question to a guest is not "What'll you drink?" but "Will you have anything in your Scotch?"

Mealtimes

Kiwis are hospitable. If they like the look of travellers met along the way they will often suggest their coming home for a meal, or even offer a bed for the night. If the invitation is "Come for tea", it is wise to say "What time?"

'Tea' for most Kiwis means a hot meal served around 5 to 6 p.m. On farms and among older people tea is usually a cold meal, a hot 'dinner' being eaten at midday. (Otherwise, an invitation to dinner means you are expected any time between 6 and 8 p.m.)

Tea can also mean afternoon tea from 3 to 4 p.m., and these days it is often coffee. The old-established smoko (workers' tea break) takes place at 10 a.m. and 3 p.m., although far fewer people now smoke, and smoking is prohibited in many public places except in specially designated areas.

"Come home for supper" means refreshments around 10 o'clock or at the end of an evening's entertainment, unless the hosts are recently back from England and have adopted the English word 'supper' for an evening meal.

It comes as a relief that lunch means simply lunch.

Staple Foods

Most families get fish and chips at least once a week – fresh and surpassingly good if bought in a coastal town – but the roast dinner, 'just like Mum used to make', remains the all-time favourite. Most of the family are at their happiest when served roast hogget (yearling lamb), gravy and mint sauce, with roast potatoes, parsnips, pumpkin and *kumara*. A green vegetable such as silverbeet (Swiss chard) may or may not have been boiled to death.

The traditional festive pudding is the cream-covered pavlova or 'pav', an airy concoction of meringue and cream named after the great ballet dancer, lavishly decorated with slices of lime-green kiwifruit. An old saying runs "You'll never get a husband unless you can make a good pav..."

Kiwifruit did not originate in New Zealand. But, like so many imports, they flourished in their adopted climate. In the early 1960s an exporter wanted to sell them in the big United States markets, but he had a problem. Those were the years of the Cold War, of extreme suspicion in the US of anything remotely pertaining to communism. Since New Zealanders had always known the fruit as 'Chinese gooseberries', such self-professed 'commie fruit' could not enter the American market. What to do?

An advertising agency was asked to come up with a list of possible new names. Name number 30 was 'kiwiberry'. The exporter pounced on it, but consulted a botanist who said, "It's not a berry. It's a fruit." And so kiwifruit was born.

Salads

Salads are the touchstones of Kiwi cuisine.

It is still quite possible to find the standard salad which adult Kiwis remember from childhood. This was invariably made of finely sliced one-variety lettuce, usually cut up hours earlier, decorated with slices of tomato, cucumber and hardboiled eggs. A cut-glass dish of sliced beetroot in vinegar might be served on the side. And that was salad. If you asked for salad, that was what you got. No more, no less. The salad dressing was made from a can of sweetened condensed milk mixed with mustard and vinegar. Vinaigrettes were unknown. Both oil and garlic were highly suspect 'foreign foods'.

Now there is an explosion of experimentation with salads. Fed by interest in vegetarianism, especially in the cities, platters boast crisp salad vegetables presented with orange, pineapple and kiwifruit, and garnished with herbs and your choice of smoked salmon, fat mussels and a range of cheeses. Magazines compete with full-colour spreads of new and seasonal dishes of every kind.

Kiwis are gradually becoming more sophisticated, but their concept of high living, of real luxury, still tends to be a chocolate wrapped in gold foil and placed on a hotel guest's pillow.

Eating Out

Dining out is a comparatively new departure for the traditional Kiwi, and is still often seen as a reward for a hard day's DIY, not as a pure pleasure in itself. A certain puritanism attaches itself to a Kiwi's pleasures.

The growth in tourism and the emergence of world-class vineyards, many with their own restaurants, has meant that large numbers of young people train as chefs, and higher standards of food preparation and presentation are slowly seeping through the population. But it will take a lot to dislodge the staple of Kiwi cuisine – the bottle of tomato sauce. The custom of the country is 'tom' sauce with everything – except ice-cream.

Systems

Kiwis like to say of adversity that it's 'character forming' This is fortunate because they are experiencing a good deal of it as they come through the biggest social upheaval in their history. The economy nearly came unstuck in the late 1970s and '80s after oil prices soared overseas. The government borrowed heavily to finance alternative fuel projects, a policy known as 'Think Big'. "Thinking far too big," grumble the normally thrifty Kiwis, still faced with huge repayments.

Something had to be done, and successive governments have used the banner of 'economic reform' to cut back New Zealand's traditional health and welfare spending to the bone. What used to be known as security from cradle to grave is now tough on the young and their parents, tough on those nearest the grave, and far from easy for those in between.

New Zealand is caught up in rapid change but, because it has a short history, most of its services and systems are fairly modern, however they may perform. This doesn't stop Kiwis from grumbling about them. It's much more fun than praising.

Health and Welfare

When Kiwis 'take sick' or are 'a bit crook', they expect to be looked after. Once they begin to recover, they are 'on the improve'. Whatever their condition, Kiwis expect not just health services, but also the provision of housing, welfare and superannuation. This expectation dates from the days when the country considered itself the social welfare laboratory of the world. Since the 1980s, governments have been trying to wean them from this foolish notion. It's an uphill battle.

For their part, the Kiwis do their best not to develop conditions requiring non-urgent surgery. Unless they have private health insurance (regarded as a damned imposition imported from the United States), they face long waiting lists for operations. Meanwhile hospitals have closed wards and reduced staff. Known as 'health reforms' or 'being competitive', it is all in the interests of saving money.

Kiwis see themselves as a nation of hunters and mountain climbers and general risk-takers, and every weekend there are enough accidents and search-and-rescue parties under way to prove it. Taking too much care of one's body goes against the pioneering spirit.

With all that sunshine, good butter, cream and fat lamb in their youth, heart disease and other effects of high cholesterol intake, plus cancer, especially melanoma, are the most feared and talked-about illnesses. Being over-weight is commonplace and weight-loss courses are booming. 'UV' (ultra violet light) is now an established word in everyday language. It is an Aussie canard that Kiwi sheep have to wear sunglasses, but sun hats and sunscreen are worn by all, and the bronzed hunks of yesteryear are looked at askance. They are either mad, or visiting Australians.

Britain's Royal Family is credited with helping to make homeopathic treatments more acceptable. Most pharmacists (still called chemists by the Kiwis) have a large range of alternative medicines. A growing number of doctors, as well as practising in the orthodox way, have an interest in homeopathy. Acupuncture is available nearly everywhere from both medical and non-medical practitioners. Healthfood stores proliferate.

These days Kiwis, as well as visitors to their country, have to pay when they consult a doctor unless they have a 'frequent user' concession. The new emphasis on individual responsibility for keeping well and thus saving the state money has led to a rash of Wellness Clinics, and this is the one aspect of the (otherwise disliked) health reforms which meets with general approval. People plan to live long, and most of them do.

Hygiene

It was said of many older male Kiwis that they used to have a bath a week, whether they needed it or not. The daily shower is now taken for granted by most people, and even unregenerate older Kiwis have stepped up the number of baths they take.

Aftershave has been grudgingly accepted by mature males, but out in the country any grooming aid other than hair cream puts the user at risk of being called a 'poofter', or a male who 'pees sitting down'.

Kiwis used to be a nation of premature denture-wearers, more because so many water supplies lacked essential minerals than because of neglect. The free and very necessary dental service for all schoolchildren was a source of national pride. Dentists were the highest earners of all professionals. Since the fluoridation of most of the water supplies, however, dental health has improved to a point where dentists, it is said, have had to sell their second yachts.

Counselling

A consultancy, support group or counselling organisation exists for almost everything.

Victim Support teams swing into action automatically after serious crimes, including burglary. A team arrived to counsel one householder after the theft of his lawnmower. He would survive the trauma, he assured them. He and his lawnmower were only on nodding terms.

Physical, mental or emotional ills, whatever the life crisis, there will be help at hand – or you can start an organisation yourself. Take the relatively new phenomenon of women who are juggling marriage and careers and who tend to postpone having children until their 30s. If they then find it difficult to conceive, they resort to fertility clinics. The heartbreak if they are unsuccessful? A support group is at hand. Twins, triplets, or even more? The support groups blossom.

Solo parents are given a living allowance by the government. Few babies are available for adoption, and many couples desperate for a child have adopted from Romanian or Russian orphanages. There are support groups all along the line. Sometimes it seems as if everyone is counselling everyone else.

Crime and Punishment

Most Kiwis are reasonably law-abiding. Corruption is rare, so it is big news indeed when people in high places are caught tax-dodging or something even more heinous. Perpetrators of white collar crime and corporations suspected of being 'on the take', or at least sailing close to the wind, are despised and resented. They are commonly believed to be putting themselves beyond the ken of everyday detective work by means of computer fraud or complex transactions off-shore. This gives them an unfair advantage over the ordinary bloke giving crime a go. It's not playing the game.

Maori are disproportionately represented in crime statistics. This is not surprising, given the high level of unemployment among Maori and the fact that half their population is under 25. The move to the towns away from the old tribal discipline also means the traditional authority of the *kaumatua,* or elders, is increasingly disregarded.

Kiwis know from films and television series that the world's police on occasion can be bad, mad and not nice to know. Kiwi cops are different. They do not carry guns unless there is real danger (there are regional armed offenders squads on alert). The most frequent contact with the constabulary is asking for directions when you are a stranger in town. If there is an accusation of police brutality or over-zealousness, more likely among the younger ranks, uproar continues until the matter is sorted out – Kiwis like their cops to be above reproach.

Prisons are referred to as 'colleges of crime': a raft of alternative punishments and rehabilitation measures attempts to keep malefactors from becoming better educated. Most of these appear to fail, and the recidivism rate remains high. Some prisons, such as Auckland's forbidding Mount Eden, might have come straight from the pages of Dickens. Others to which non-violent first offenders are sent are called 'country clubs' by those for whom revenge, not rehabilitation, is the byword. A passionately-led movement exists for restorative justice. Here the offender is brought face to face with the victim in a controlled situation with the dual aim of trying to make it up to the victim in some way as well as getting the perpetrator to face up to wrong-doing.

Education

Farseeing Kiwis take care to ensure their children are born at the end or beginning of the school year, December or February, or at least near the beginning of a school term. Children may begin school on their fifth birthday, and most do. It is, therefore, less confusing for everyone if their arrival is at the beginning of a term.

There was a time when every primary school child in the country began and ended each of the year's three terms on the same day. Now both primary and secondary systems have four terms a year with individual schools deciding on their term dates. For families with children at different schools, the school holidays can be a nightmare of trying to find common ground for time-honoured trips away. School buses transport pupils back and forth, and a Correspondence School teaches the truly isolated.

Before the children are born there is provision for their parents to be educated in aspects of childbirth and child rearing. This is done mainly through hospitals and a network of parents centres which also offer support during the pre-school stage. Plunket rooms are a feature of every town. The Plunket Society (named after Lord Plunket, a Governor-General and first patron) has a national system of Plunket nurses and voluntary committees dedicated to advising on the feeding and general care of babies and toddlers. Play centres, kindergartens and the successful *kohanga reo* (literally 'language nests') for Maori and Pacific Island children, are widely accepted as essential preparation for school itself.

Ongoing stratagems, such as work experience, attempt to keep all children busy at school, and to some extent the compulsory learning of Maori language and culture has succeeded, and not just with Maori youngsters. Many non-Maori elect to study these subjects longer than the required minimum, especially as Maori is the country's second official language. Young people, particularly Pacific Islanders and Maori, who leave school with no qualifications face a shrinking employment pool.

A new system called Tomorrow's Schools was designed ostensibly to give parents more say in their children's education. Cunningly, it also reduces government costs, since parents have to take over much of the administration and fundraising. At school fairs it is often said, "Bet they didn't use cake stalls to fund the navy." Schools in wine-making areas use parents' wine-making skills. As a fundraiser, it beats cakes.

Transport

Whether it is plane, train, coach or the popular ferries which link the North and South Islands, long-distance public transport is generally reliable and reasonably priced.

Not so public transport within cities. Bus services have been so reduced in numbers and routes that you are unlikely to get anywhere near where you want to go when you want to get there. The city councils have made the reductions to save money, but this does not prevent them continually haranguing their citizens about the advantages of taking the bus.

Christchurch, dead flat except for its guardian Cashmere Hills, is the city of bicycles. Wellington, its harbour rimmed by hills, has cable cars and more than a quarter of the country's mountain bikes. Auckland has the worst transport problems. Its proud harbour bridge was not able to cope with all the traffic and an entire extra section, pre-fabricated in Japan, had to be attached to the side to provide more vehicle lanes. It is known as the Nippon Clip-on.

Large-scale imports of cheap, used vehicles from Japan, on top of the traditional imports, enable most Kiwis to own a car, sometimes two or three to a family. Kiwis love cars, no matter how old. It's a reaction to all that walking in the early days.

Young people can get a probationary driving licence when they are 15. This is considered too young for today's traffic conditions, but it is a hangover from the past when people began their working lives at the age of 14 or 15.

Instead of lollipop men and women shepherding schoolchildren over road crossings, Kiwi children do it themselves. Road safety officers groom them in the proper procedures, and it is a great honour for ten-year-olds and older to take their turn in charge of zebra crossings (with a teacher to supervise). Adults, remembering these road safety drills from their own schooldays, are careful to co-operate.

Accident statistics underline the need for basic safety regulations. New Zealand's scenery is so breathtaking, and many of the roads traverse such rugged countryside, that when you are overcome by the beauties of nature, the rule is to pull well off the road and stop. Cries of wonder at mountain, lake or river have led to catastrophe when eyes have strayed from the road ahead.

But the road toll continues to rise and the number of roadside crosses goes on increasing. Kiwis consider it a Fair Go for the police to erect warning notices in areas where speed cameras are operating. Motorists duly slow down, then speed up again when they reckon they have left the danger zone behind.

Government

At first glance the mechanisms of government look simple.

There is one Parliament with no Upper House. A Governor-General (New Zealand has had its first woman in this post) represents the British Crown, and the country is an ardent and loyal member of the British Commonwealth. The notion of moving towards a republic, put forward by a prime minister of Irish descent, does not get much support – so far.

Every Kiwi citizen from the age of 18 has the vote, and there is one set of laws for the whole country – none of your Aussie-type separate states' legislation here.

Voting may be simple, but the country is in turmoil as it tries to come to terms with the implications of its new voting system, MMP or Mixed Member Proportional representation.

MMP represents the biggest-ever change in New Zealand's political system, and it has all come about because of Kiwi devotion to a Fair Go.

Kiwis voted in a referendum for MMP because they believed successive governments of left and right had moved far beyond their mandates when tackling ways of reducing the country's debt. Once in power, politicians seemed to favour certain sections of the community over others, a sin in a country which believes in equality of opportunity. The gap between the haves and have-nots grew too wide for Kiwi consciences. MMP was brought in to give greater choice, to allow everyone to be represented.

Previously an election was a straight one-vote system, the winner being the first past the post. With MMP, each citizen has two votes. One is for the electoral candidate, the other is for one of the registered political parties and is known as the list vote. The more list votes a party gets, the more parliamentary seats it is entitled to.

One aim is a 'culture of consensus', to give minority viewpoints a fair hearing. But the tail could even end by wagging the dog if the major parties are so desperate to build alliances that they make big concessions to a small possible ally. On the other hand, the large number of small parties all wanting to have a go could mean that none gets an electorate seat or the minimum 5% of votes needed to qualify.

It's a changing scene, and all these possibilities make Kiwis uneasy. It's just as well there's legal provision for another referendum to change MMP if it doesn't fulfil expectations. Achieving a Fair Go has never been easy.

Business

Bosses and Workers

Kiwi bosses like to say that they are workers too. Most businesses are small, everyone is on first name terms and formality is minimal.

Kiwis grumble about work but get more upset if they don't have any. Because of the considerable unemployment, government schemes provide financial inducements to employers, such as subsidised wages, to give the unemployed a taste of working life. Most firms also give work experience to older secondary school students.

Women overall are paid less and hold far fewer senior positions than men. The widespread celebrations in 1993 of the first 100 years of women's suffrage have not yet translated in the workplace into opportunities which are actually equal. Supporters of the women's movement know this is because men are slow to see women's superior ability. They like to sport a matter-of-fact bumper sticker which says quite simply, 'Boys Are Dumb'.

Business people load themselves with cell phones, fax machines, laptop computers and modems. These artifacts of the modern age are the direct descendants of that piece of number eight fencing wire – the best available tool for the job at the time.

Exports

It is all very well making things in factories and growing more on farms, but there are so few Kiwis that they cannot sell enough at home and have to go in for exporting.

Wool, lamb and butter used to be the staple exports. Now they are joined by a wide range of goods from computer software to quality foodstuffs. New Zealand wines make up a small but significant part of the country's exports.

In a free market there can be some rather extraordinary goings-on. One Kiwi skipper of a trans-Tasman freighter, asked what his main cargo was, replied deadpan, "We take our cheesecake over to Oz, and we bring their cheesecake back here."

The exporters' main problem, after getting the world to know just where New Zealand is, is getting the message over that it is the home of high-quality products as well as being a great place to visit. A campaign called 'The New Zealand Way' has the specific task of overcoming both these problems. Basic to the campaign is the idea that here is a youthful country with fresh and experimental ways of approaching things. (If you don't have generations of experience, you might as well try to capitalise on the fact.) It was one of their own, Lord Rutherford, the first person to split the atom, who pointed out that if you come from a small country without much money, then you have to think.

'Brand New Zealand' is the New Zealand Way logo, a silver fern placed diagonally across a clean, green New Zealand, set in an ocean of blue. Kiwis who provide goods and services which meet its standards are entitled to use the marketing forces mustered behind this image.

One of the many inventive manufacturers who fit neatly into this whole concept lives in a lovely bay in the beautiful Queen Charlotte Sound. He is a designer who keeps in touch by fax and cellphone, thus having the best of all worlds. Each day he travels across the Sound with his partner-wife and school-going children to their small factory in the mainland village. There they produce Naiad inflatable boats built to their own design – boats which are sought-after by coastguard and sea sports officials the world over. Kiwis took extra pleasure in watching their yacht win the America's Cup because the little boats buzzing around and zipping officials through the waters of San Diego were Naiads.

Tourism

'Sustainable tourism' is a catch phrase among Kiwis. The country has become so popular a tourist destination, there is concern that visitors will not be able to see the clean green track through the bush because of the sheer number of others trying to see it too.

Fortunately, empty space is what the Kiwi still has lots of, enough and to spare. In a land mass only a little bigger than the United Kingdom and a little smaller than Japan, mountains, lakes, rivers, bush reserves and geo-thermal areas trip over one another.

For most people few things beat a boat ride along one of the many rivers. And it is the icing on the cake or the froth on the water if they know that the jetboat they are riding in is another Kiwi invention – even if they get tipped out of it at the next rapids. It's all just part of the pioneering experience.

The latest development caters to nature of a different sort. To counter criticism that all there is on offer is the beauty and variety of the scenery, grandiose casinos have been established. Kiwis appear to be the main patrons. Visitors are too busy looking at the view.

Language and Accent

Strange words and signs bemuse the visitor to New Zealand. In public bars in the north of the country there is apt to be a notice saying 'No Patches'. This has nothing to do with a requirement for new clothing. Patches are gang regalia and likely to provoke a fight.

Farther south a billboard might proclaim, 'Old Man's Beard Must Go'. It is not meant to discriminate. Old Man's Beard is an imported variety of clematis which, like other imports ranging from thistles to gorse, thrives so well in New Zealand that it threatens to strangle the native bush.

Spoken sentences often end on a rising inflection, especially if they have the matey 'eh' tacked on to them. 'We're going to the pictures, eh.'

Honest, or perhaps just better-informed, Kiwis will admit their country has borrowed many of its colloquialisms from Australia. Linguistic experts, however, say it is a two-way trade and that the Aussie accent is beginning to be affected by the New Zealand one, which as every Kiwi knows is much more refined.

Fish 'n chips, say the experts, comes out as fush 'n chups from Kiwi lips, whereas the Aussies say feesh 'n cheeps, as in the name of their largest city, Seedney.

Vowel sounds can be a trap. The story is told of the Kiwi hostess who telephoned to invite an American businessman to bring his wife to stay in her unfinished home, still uncarpeted, and with bare concrete floors.

"I warn you," she said, "it's pretty basic. There may be sacks on the floor." There was a slight pause, then the gallant American came back with an accommodating, "Sex on the floor, sex anywhere."

The Author

Christine Cole Catley says she hadn't realised what good Kiwi qualifications she has until she came to write this book.

A fifth generation New Zealander, she has forebears from England and Scotland and one Swedish great-grand-father. Most of them were sheep farmers and she grew up on a North Island sheep farm not far from the small town named after another of her great-grandfathers, James Bull. It is 'the only place where you can get milk from bulls'.

She went to university in the South Island, spent most of her working life in Wellington as a journalist, advertising copywriter (it was she who came up with the name kiwiberry), television critic, broadcaster and teacher of journalism, then went south again.

Like many New Zealanders she is able to live and work in a beautiful but remote place – in her case the Marlborough Sounds – because of today's communication technology. There she works as a book publisher, writes, reads, gardens, drives a 1973 Triumph (rather past its 'use by' date), and goes out on the water whenever she can.

That's when she's not travelling. Her three children all live overseas, and she is on her fourth passport.